ORPHANOTROPHIA

poems by

ANDREW KOZMA

For my mother, Judith Dicus, and my brother, Jason Kozma

Orphanotrophia

CONTENTS

PART THREE

PART FOUR

ORPHANOTROPHIA

…and doth not all to go so strangely with familiar pain in the old way?

{William Hope Hodgson, *The Night Land*}

PART ONE

SONG OF THE TRAVELER

Never sit at the front of the bus. Never be the first
to get off.

Never be the first to give in to pleasure or to admit pain.
Let your shoes

wear out your feet. Let blisters sing your praises. Let holes
become your saints.

This is the road to Desolation Row. You can turn back.
No one needs to know.

ODE TO THE COMMON HOUSEFLY

O Eternal Worrier, you strive to lick
your prints from every surface. O Six-Legged God,
O Tiny Resurrectionist, if I begged
you to stop, would you stop, would you nod

your clockwork head, would you promise to rot
in the corner after I've squashed you, silent
and uneager to raise your children from the dead?
Perhaps you aren't to blame, O Careless Parent.

You sow your seed only where it takes,
and I left the dishes uncleansed, the fruit
clogging the trash with its seductive scent.
Dogged Companion, you wear your dark suit

with pride, eager to mourn whatever dies.
I'm not your friend! You're not mine! What lies
we tell. I love the living, and you, the dead.
And here we are again, breaking bread.

SIX YEARS LATER, THE MEMORY OF THE RAW FISH CUBES CONTINUED TO HAUNT HER

{from a line by Anne Lamott}

The ice in her water pinks with sunset. The coral-blue
of the glass in uncertain light. Everything is dying

all the time. Just after being caught, the dull knife
scattering jewels over the bloodstained wood. Skin slides off

as easily as clothing, under an expert hand. The raw sex of it,
eating whole pieces of another life. Bones thrown to the ocean,

guts washed free with the rain, there is no record
except in her body. So quick the beheading, the eyes still quivered.

ODE TO THE PARASITIC WASP

O Belly-buster, O Laugher at Tragedies,
you slip your young beneath our skin, organ-bound

life-lusters, distaff worms to do us in.
O Socialite, O Stalker, O Delicate Chitin Flower,

you plant the unwanted pearls in the oysters of the world.
Your young growl the stomach into life. Indigestion

or digestion? No need to spike my blood to silence.
I am willing! Childless, I will transmogrify!

O Hovering Mother, O Abandonment, I squirm
inside, chewing my way free – hundreds of Is

eager for the sky and desperate, O Midwife,
for the end of me.

ODE TO THE SOFT TICK

Soft ticks were put to a sinister purpose as recently as 100 years ago by the Turkman and Uzbek tribes. They were used for a form of execution called Khiva Khanate in which prisoners were chained to a wall or a bed in a cell into which specially bred ticks were introduced in huge numbers. Since the ticks had been starved first, it was a slow and agonizing death.

{*The Life that Lives on Man*, Michael Andrews}

O Loving Needle, O Blood Bag, all that's in my heart
will fill you as a woman fills a dress, her hair roped

in a lock-tight fist. O Unsquashable Hope, the woman
laughs outside these walls in the sputtering sunlight

like a dog who enjoys the attention of being beaten.
O Many-armed Masseuse, I enjoy your attention

like the sulphurous tap-water guzzled by the man
too long on the streets, shoved away from every shaded alley,

fortunate to find this abandoned house. I will be your house,
O Hungry Pilgrim, I will be your dress. Fill me.

SONG OF THE REENACTOR

We are in Southern soil and we breathe with the worms
the blood-drunk dirt. Why kill anyone

if there's a chance of an empty afterlife?
Monuments to that emptiness surround us. A ditch

meant to hide an army, become its grave. The carmine rust
of cannons left untended, their work done.

Our work is the act of memory. We become the gravestones
and, oh, the crowds come and go,

trampling dry grass into shattered brown bones
and flowers scar the hills with blue and yellow and purple,

beautiful as a storm, these common weeds. History tells us

so much less than we imagined, so much more
than we can understand.

THIS IS NOT OUR DAY

The air is on fire with kittens.
My mailbox is full of black holes.
The highway is drenched in mint julep.
The mountains have nowhere to go.

The trees drank all the whiskey.
The itch decided to stay.
A fortune buried ambition.
Cinnamon smells of the grave.

SONG OF THE SELF-RIGHTEOUS

Like a cooking show where the oven-cradled food
emerges smoking into the air, ruined, but still

the guests are encouraged to taste. Nothing so sweet
as food you don't have to eat. Nothing so kind

as enduring what you don't mind. O Bland Heroes,
there is work to be done! There are numbers to run

and stats to compile! How many have died?
And was it worth their while? If it ain't broken,

let's break it, said the sharks to the fishes.
There's an end to suffering, but we don't want it.

SONG OF THE MIGRAINED

Head like dynamite socketed to a coal seam
rumbling the earth to a crumble, stumbling

miners' feet with dumb purpose. O Porpoise,
you nose the shark from its living stupor

into death, smiling every step of the way.
O Purpose, who gave you the reason to live?

O Life, what gives with this pain stapled
to my temple like Jesus himself rants incoherent?

O Lord, O Neurologist, what debasement my body enjoys,
what storage for suffering, this device I am?

SONG OF THE PSYCHOPATH

My head is a tympanum. The world is an orchestra.
Nature is the instruments turning inside out.

My head tries, but it can't make enough noise
to drown out the noise. My head is going about this all wrong.

Owl heads never have this problem. But my head
is narrow and agrees that space and time are fixed

to a single point in the distance. I am standing there,
watching my head slowly approach, beating its drum

of warning. For so long I've been without you,
and I've been okay. Silent, but okay. Thoughtless, too,

but, oh, how my instincts have raged erotic! The brain,
dear head, sees only the death of each moment it lives.

My head nods. It agrees. It opens its mouth to let me in.

CIGARETTE BURNS

On your skin, the perfect circle I once heard
only the insane can make. If I touch the scar,

am I culpable for its healing? Better to look away.
Better to take a picture and explore your wounds in private.

O Love, there's no such thing as love, just this record
written in your flesh that we can't forget. A skin graft

is a new set of clothes unable to hide your damned swagger.
O Dentist! O Plastic Surgeon! O Psychiatrist! Hide me

beneath me so deep I'll never be found. Leave me coffined
in a world of seems. If all we are is illusion, then your body

is a cocoon and we'll be forgiven for what we've done.
But if God holds the camera, he'll let the film run.

PART TWO

SONG OF THE SINGLE-MINDED

The ants scent their future, one-by-one,
the planes divide the sky, blood
pushes through darkness until light calls it up
through a needle, ocean currents drag life
in an endless loop of reproduction,
monarch wings litter the earth
in mile-long swaths of poisonous color,
each virus fills a cell with itself until
the cell explodes, grass reaches through
the soil in bud after bud, poking its crown
through the ground until the original dies
and all that's left are copies and a bald spot
in the yard, and eventually you are so far away
there is no trace of where you came from.

EVERY SNOWFLAKE WILL HAVE ITS OWN NAME

When I was born, thousands of others breathed their first.
I crawled the tile floor and fed the dust my skin,
and then became friends with the insects. They rattled

their names to me. I picked them up and shook them
like toys until they pieced apart and mom cleaned up the mess.
The world is our plaything or we are the playthings of the world.

O Playboy of the Western World, O Ambassador of Riches,
where is the key to your kingdom, and why am I
trapped in it? This ramshackle home I call my body

won't let me leave. Its halls echo with voices
and the voices echo with names. Every single one of us
is unique and must be labeled so. Ipso facto.

ELVIS

Prince of Paupers, we all wish a hillbilly's heaven:
overgrown hills awash with honey and buzzing with the young

of every species, and love in the air like a mist so thick
your clothes are sodden the second you leave your ramshackle house

to rot in unforgiving memory. If I had a dollar for every dream of fame
deferred, every musician turned electrician, every sculptor

turned dietician, every writer lost to law and a love of words
straight-jacketed into a single meaning! O Lonely Boy of Hip-Swung Song,

maybe it's better to die young. At that age, all the promise
of promise. We don't let flowers grow old before dressing our tables

with their beautiful corpses. And we don't let our animals go to seed
before we feast. Why not leave us in a burst of flame? Why not lie

in state forever, glass-coffined, lips sneered for a kiss? O King Ghost,
there is no building waiting for your leave to leave. You are in our minds.

And no matter how hard you try, you will never, ever die.

SONG OF THE FORECLOSER

The walls are thin as puddle ice. The carpets twitch with lice.
Today, we'll divorce this house from its prior life.

An oak chest stuffed with oak. Closets soaked
with hollow moths and packed roach eggs.

What gouges result from years of wearing.
A touch, however gentle, strips the finish.

I'll oil every ghosting hinge, replace every mirror
with a new silvered face, polish the hardwoods

until each screams, *Stay with me! Without you
I'm nothing!* A grace note, a death mask, a scar.

SONG OF THE GHOST HUNTER

If there was a ghost, he's gone now and no one
can hurt you. If you were a ghost,
you'd be gone now, too. This house is a ghost,

and in its walls ghost organs blush without blood.
If you peel the tile up, ghost wood
splinters into your fingers, encysting like memories.

If only the house had been sold, then we would see
each other for who we were,
though bodies are the ghosts of our previous cells,

and those of us are never coming back. If a ghost,
then something once, living.
If in a certain light, I can see through my flesh.

If in the dark I can see nothing at all. If you come,
ghost, you can rescue yourself.
If I hold my breath till it aches, I rescue us both.

THE WARD

If we claim the world is round, we're insane.
If we prove the world is round, we're burned at the stake. The world
is flat. Oh, what mistakes we'll make.

ODE TO THE CINNAMON-COVERED WAXWORM

O Fueling Fire, O Snack on Legs, you wormed your way
into the pan, blind as all worms are. Which is to say,
not blind at all. Burdened by senses as Atlas was the world,

you smelled the oil, you felt its heat. You thought, *At last,*
here is something good to eat! Tiny black legs, tiny black head,
it's hard to believe you're dead. You lay in my palm like a pill.

But then you dressed yourself in spices and sweet-scent.
I saw with the eyes of the grackle and wrinkled my snout.
An animal. Just an animal. Your body split

upon my tongue. What have I done? The brain recoils
but the body rejoices. There are not enough pleasures
in this world, Love, and we must exploit every one.

ODE TO THE LOVE BUG

O Unthreatening Sex Fiend, climb your gendered body-twin
and strive to futurize. Four days alive (a little more

if male) is barely time enough for love, or even death.
But, O Fragile Gloves, how you throw your bodies into it!

In smokes of thousands, you dress the baking highway
and declare your passion to every passing glass. Do you see

yourself eternal? Even as you die, your angel-self in air
declares another love affair, and those two, too,

are crushed against the grill of this fine day. O Girl, come with me
and love as only insects can. Let us be reborn

a hundred times an hour to fresh our faces to each other's lips.
O Tiny Fuckers, teach us to let the world consume us.

SONG OF THE STARVING

I am eating this page as you read it.
I am rolling up the road as you drive it.

My belly is a faerie hill enticing all inside,
though none may leave. My iron grip

is made of broken ribs. The gristle of my body
is too tough to chew, so the world pretends I have skin,

that I am not an organ wheezing in the sterile air.
O Hunger, the only god I've ever known, whose vise-like hands

perfect my stomach, who strives for the Platonic,
your presence in the world proves we are too far gone.

There is no forgiveness. There is no hope.
There is my open mouth, my swollen tongue.

ODE TO THE MALE HONEYBEE

...and the few hundred fat male drones with big eyes whose sole purpose—so far as we know—is to have sex with the queen on her single mating flight and who, ultimately, as winter approaches and food resources dwindle, will be dragged from the hive by the workers, expelled to starve or, if resistant, stung to their death.

{Hugh Raffles, *Insectopedia*}

Push yourselves into the air, O Cheap Blossoms, and flirt
with the dirt. For a single purpose are you made, O One-Trick Honeys,

and for that matter you are fed, you are housed, you are suffered.
But when the going gets tough, O Wide-Eyed Fluff, the weak

shall inherit the earth. Sadly, there is no food there. You crowd
the brittle grass with your bodies, eager for what warmth you had no chance

to give. O Once-Treasured, your more resilient fellows follow you down,
their love-stung corpses a grand parade in honor of might've-been.

What did you expect? Other hungry beasts crowd around. They teethe
your little limbs. Give it up! Give it up! They taste your honeyed breath.

ODE TO THE DYING MOTH

Taste the honeycomb of light, this hive of brightness
enclosing you like a cage. Free to roam the tides of night,

you settle for the porch and the bulb that blooms
like an echo of the moon. O Bitter-Wing, O Piecemeal Ghost,

I can't save you. There are too many porches, each with eyes
behind the shades admitting there are too many porches,

and what's the use blessing this one alone with darkness?
O Martyr of Dust, O Farmer of the Forgotten, O Consumer

of All We've Discarded, your wings smudge my palms in fury.
O Living Wick, the floor is littered with your fellows.

OUR TRASH AND THE TRASH OF OTHERS

This animal tail is devoid of animal. It is clean and decorative,
the blood dyeing the sides of the drainage ditch,
the echo of violence. Some coyote was here,
some falcon artiste concerned with only its own creation.

But nothing now, except me and this mystery unfolded.
Wyoming is a silent expanse. Emptiness and the wind
the only other inhabitants. But evidence is everywhere: deer
pellets, cow patties, splotches of white-and-black bird dung.

I am alone, and I am responsible. No yips or bird cries
to take credit for this tail, only proof of the animal
that was. I will not bury it. In the grass
a beer can shines like an arrogant, forgotten tooth.

NUTRIENT CYCLING THROUGH THE BIOMASS

Gnaw at the heart of the Earth, Great Worm of Waste,
and core us a home in the burning innards. When the sun dies

we will not die with it. Just because the universe pretends
to end is no reason for us to, and in the utter dark

I will hold you close and tell you stories of the light.
In this ghost-of-the-future city we live in, trash promises

resurrection. A rotten tomato, a chicken skin, bread molded over
into something new and alive, all of the organic transcribes

itself into the mulling ground. And the greasy plastic, the rusting metal,
they, too, disintegrate into the soil. Like the stone and shell in sand,

each handful of dirt contains microscopic copies of its origins,
tiny tin cans, shopping bags, and the faces of the self-effacing dead.

AS HE HAD NO ISSUE, THE TITLE BECAME EXTINCT ON HIS DEATH

The air is wet and yellow. It crumbles like ash
from a discarded cigarette. There is rain incoming.

There is concrete incoming. Tomorrow I will sleep with the fishes
who never sleep, the sharks who never stop swimming,

the lies that never stop being believed. Time-lapsed,
the world falls to pieces. My yellowed teeth

corrupt my breath. I once believed in immortality,
at least one thing unending, but all that exists

can be both created and destroyed. In the empty lot,
wildflowers rampage and the foundation disintegrates.

SONG OF THE SUICIDE

The compost brings growth to the garden. Every rotting body
drags itself into the earth.

Cremation is for those afraid of their flesh falling to ribbons,
streaming through hairy grass,

a festival for the end of the day. The sun gives itself over to storms
to imagine the scoured face revealed

when the rain ends and, heat-kissed, the world steams into newness.
Rawness. Salt of the earth where nothing grows.

The open wound of a rain-glazed empty highway. That highway
narrowed for construction to one choked lane,

but the only car is yours. Miles and miles of no exits, and the only car
is yours. The doors lock. The car is yours.

STARMAN

The man says, *We are not who we were*
and never will be again. But who's this we? And who are you

to give me such a clownish talking to?
O Stars That Fall to Earth, who asked you down? Who wanted angelskins

to dress ourselves in? Good doctors,
if bonescrews exist, what held us together before? What Prometheus

sidestepped God to add the self
to our consciousness? And why now choose to let the boulder fall

without intending to roll it back up?
What of the towns crushed under its wheel? How can you prove ants

are less than we? Is your proof
they scream less loudly? *Stop,* the man says, *asking questions.*

The stars are stitched together
with the thread of our desire. O Love, you lost me to death

long before we were born.
Yet when there's a knock, hopeful always, you open the door.

PART THREE

PULGAS VESTIDAS

Even our smallest pains we dress up. Even our gentlest scrapes
hurt, or we want them to hurt, or we want people
to believe they hurt. There's the rub,

the want. Our parasites are part of us, and what a beautiful, skeletal part.
These fleas garbed as bride and groom, as lovers (we hope)
frozen in a matchbox as folk art.

How did they sew such small clothes? How did they sleeve their limbs?
When did they get our blood in their mouths,
the two of us made one in them?

INTO A MODE OF EXCESS

I was offered a hand and I took it. But three hands were not enough.
A successful life with a single head is an optimist's dream. All transplants

are proof of failure and this templated body is now a template for others.
The Hindu gods had it right. A dozen arms, an elephant head, the body accepted

for its exceptions. The Greeks prized Argus, he of the hundred eyes,
and when each was excised with a small knife, he was revered for the oracles

of ignorance that remained. Speak in tongues with your many tongues. Say my name
until it becomes meaningless, until all you hear is your heart's dialogue with your
blood.

Royalty was marked with a six-fingered hand. So much more secure the grasp
on what makes us betters. Where's the tail evolution stole? Our extra teeth

gone obsolete? We are less than we were. Once, I counted every bone in my body,
each to each. They added up, but still I found myself wanting.

THE BOXING MATCH

{based on Edward Hart's taxidermic dioramas}

O Grand Schemes of Bully Taxidermists, dead on arrival, glories faded
before you've set knife to skin, skin to needle, needle to thread,

Hart will have none of you! Death is not the end, but the beginning
of creation. The corpses, those shelled children of God, eyes bright

with glass, strong bones wired into a pose that will never tire,
they rise again, resurrected and perfected. These ground squirrels,

commonest of common pests, tree rats, attic conquerors, in death
become lithe boxers, white-shorts clad, red gloves at the ready, proud

hearts through their chests seen pounding, tiny fixed grins ferocious,
cannibalistic. Heretic Hart, you usurped God's dreams. O Dreamer,

the truth is so banal. So stick out your chin, accept the blow to the jaw.
Even the viscera, carefully deposed from their throne, feed the flies.

BODY BAGS

Morgue man, cadaverous tooth, smile unhinged
at the cocoon before you. Inside that silk robe

lies a body unpleasant to look upon, but it's your job
to ferry all corpses from womb to grave.

Do not speak of the soul. Our spirits
preserve our flesh and good humor, but fail

at keeping us alive. O Cloud of Flies,
O Deathwatch Beetle, you are the man every man

wants to be, birthing citizens of the final world.
What remains tells a story, but that story is an end.

Sad-mouthed man, the born butterfly ruins the body
of the dead caterpillar. What a loss. Hurt heart,

properly preserved, our skins will last forever.

PRO-LIFE

Outside the window, a worm lies drying in the sun. This hospital
is my only tether to this life. The ancient Greeks believed corruption
brought life into the world, bees burgeoning into the air

from a ripe corpse, their clockwork buzz the seed of honey
unearthed from rotten lungs. The white worm turns brown, then black
and brittle as a cough. O Carpenter, your creations live on

despite the flaws in their construction. I believe no one wants
to die, they just want an end to the show, but every bit player
must act as though they're the lead. I could have saved that worm.

Instead, I waited for the bird that never came. I can only decide
for the living, and even there I err on the side of reason.
No reason to interfere. No reason to care. O Reasonable

World, stop and stare at this spineless creation! What rises
from the worm's dead flesh? O Cocoon for the Spirit,
O Soul-Rich Death, give me a concrete burial. Put this mind to rest.

AGNOLO THE FAT, AGNOLO THE LUCKY

And I, Agnolo di Tura, called the fat, buried my wife and five children with my own hands.

{Agnolo di Tura}

But, by God, I live! My fat has whittled to bone
and the sky shorn itself of clouds. There is no glory

in the sun dying behind the mountains, confident
in resurrection. All spring, grass peeled its carcass from the dirt

to stand with the flower as its bride. All this summer, the air stank
with fear of the coming plague. There is no more fear. Fickle Mistress,

the stench remained to remind us what we'll never again enjoy.
O Siena, my city of wool and wolves, you are clad in rags, and we

are the rags. I have buried the flowers and the grass under the dirt
from which they came. My hands mud-caked, I wandered

from end to end of your lonely, golden streets. God, I live,
and everyone around me praises your name.

SONG OF THE CALLING BACK

Instead, Parsons immediately threw himself into a magickal project to call down
an elemental to take her place.
{William H. Patterson, Jr., *Robert A. Heinlein, Vol. I*}

The dark clouds roiling above us are the roof of the world
because we must contain ourselves. If you have died

and I have seen your body burnt to ash and the ash
fed to the ground, then you are still alive.

Science has no answer that magic cannot duplicate, Love,
so I can reengineer you good as new. Somewhere there is a box

that has never been opened. Everything we see changes at our looking
and changes again when we look away. I am looking away.

Soon you will be behind me. Soon you will touch me. Soon
the roof will split like a cocoon, the wind will breathe your breath,

and I will not look. I will not look. But you will say, *Please.*

SONG OF THE SKYDIVER

The city is a river of noise, and I am blind
under the water. O Loving Trucks, what big fins you have

to grill me with. Noise is simply too much information
at exactly the right time to crowd your mind.

Take a clue from the clouds, miles between them
they play charades. They hold their bodies

up to the heavens, while we are crawfish
in a thirty-pound bag, our pressed-up shells clacking

telegrams our minds can't understand. The physical essence
is what we want, our brains gone on holiday and conscience

as relevant as a morality play. The most animal animal
hugs the ground where it belongs. And such a gulf

between the earth and the clouds. We are the fleas of the world.
So give me that empty and vast space. Give me a place to fall.

TRIED AND FAILED

All the Niagara barrelers shocked
at their disintegrating shells,
the ships foundering the edge

of the known world, bodies
decorating the deck, barnacles
of ruin, the factories and farms

abandoned to the elements all of us,
arm in arm, could never tame.
The ants, at least, have their excuse

of utter mindlessness, scent-drawn
along the landscape, tireless
rebuilders of their shoe-scuffed hill.

The West, too, is full of broke-tooth fences
drawn around paper homesteads
long buried in the earth.

What hopes they had, train-fed
cross-country, land burning
gold under the unchecked sun.

SONG OF THE SURVEYOR

The palm tree has spider legs for leaves.
Birds disappear in the branches, and bones

litter the concrete like cigarette butts.
O City of Transformation, dissolve me

into the tar that patches your streets,
let the squirrels line their nests with my hair.

The hands of my ancestors wave from each corner,
though you are young, your buildings impatient

to house ghosts. Your version of history
is that there is no history. O Sisyphean City,

no matter your hummingbird heart, from here
there is nowhere to go. Take me with you.

SONG OF THE COMING TO TERMS WITH IT

First, the bargaining. Then the begging. And, at last, the realization
there's no one in the room but you.

There are no terms to be had. No concessions to be won. Waiting for death
isn't as lonely as death, but only just.

In Wales there's a pot they put the dead in. The dead boil and twist
their limbs into life, but are still dead.

And then there's that philosophical fear that you're the only real one here,
everyone else an automaton. Dead.

When every tree laces the ground with the dead. When the tall grass frays
and refuses to die. When storms don't rain.

There is no it. Nothing to fear. Nothing to fight. Just the possibility of absence
and, eventually, its absence.

PART FOUR

KAREN GREENLEE

For years, I believed in death
because I, too, was dead. You can know you are feeling

and still not feel, all your nerves
assembled in some outsourced factory, off-brand Nikes called Nikos

whose only purpose is to deceive.
They fit your feet fine at first, but soon you're walking on a beach of salt.

They grow holes. They lose their soles.
This is what it's like to have sex with the dead. Their skin, at first,

is smoother than you imagine
and smells of earth. Their hair embraces your fingers like the wind,

so soft and sure. The body accepts
all of you, no matter how broken you are. It will never judge.

ORPHANOTROPHIA

Where have all the parents gone? O Children,
visiting hours are over and you must embrace the blankets.

When the lights go out, the machines take over, whispering
a Morse code of beeps and hums. They are cold metal,

but under their layered shell is a heart that will not stop
until you pull the plug. Children, you are not alone—a relief—

though you are abandoned. The windows to the world
are clean as a skeleton, but the stars are so far away.

The stars are so close. They, too, are bedded down
in the softest dark where the beating of another heart

is felt as the faintest illumination on the skin. O Orphans,
don't be afraid that no one will come for you. I am here

to admit we are all afraid—doctors, nurses, patients, parents—
that what we call life is only waiting for the night to end.

SONG OF THE BLIND

My mouth has been sealed for years
waiting for your lips. Your eyes are the doors

I've never closed. I only sleep
when my skin touches your skin.

Our bodies are echoes in an endless room.
I become the sound of your voice.

ODE TO THE MOLTING CICADA

O Treasure Hunter! O Archaeologist! You bury the years
with your brittle body, mandibles dirt-clogged. O Unspoken Voice,

you hoarse the evening with sleepy sex songs, barely awakened,
a fire engine stumbling the air. You kiss the trees.

You flutter-buzz-shiver, sidewalk-bound by my shoe, gray-green
monstrosity, friendly horror, late-night booty call.

O Unpacked Box, O Encrypted Animal,
hack yourself into something new. A dog-end

between my fingertips, a Christmas ornament.
O Life Clinger! O Bird Feeder! O Emptying Skin!

DARK STAR (DIRECTOR'S CUT)

The bomb has a loving touch. It skins with a tailor's grace,
undressing you to reveal the beauty no one ever sees.

This is what the bomb likes to believe. It ignores rumors
that the body comes apart like a puppet snipped of all its string,

and what is left, in variegated piles, is what was there all along,
all the meat and bone, nothing more, nothing less. The bomb is not heartless.

Okay, it is. The bomb admits it is. But, see, the bomb loves you.
It loves every part of you, from your lips to your ass, from your blood

to your shit, there is no bit of you the bomb will not kiss.
No clump of snot, no knot of cancer in the spleen. No, the bomb knows

there is nothing in this world that's clean. The bomb is heartless
because it is a heart, and you are what it pumps. What love it takes

to transubstantiate the body. What deceit to believe it's giving you up.

GHOSTS OF MARS

There is so much emptiness for sound to travel through.

Mars stares like a sleep-deprived eye down my telescope. What's scarier:
a disembodied eye tabulating my every move or an entire planet
as desolate as a parking lot? Lowell dressed Mars in canals,

but that was just another lie, a trick of the eye like a wedding ring
missing from a finger. The absence of proof is proof of something,
I'm sure of it, just as the absence of life is what gives life meaning.

What gives? The ghosts of Mars aren't the remnants of the dead,
but of the never-lived. They never-ate and they never-drank
and never-studied the blue-green ball below them.

They never-raised their voices to us. They never-hated us.

HEAVEN AND EARTH

So perfect is his reproduction of a whole and normal man that no one who examines
him in a clinical setting can point out in scientific or objective terms why, or how, he
is not real.

{Dr. Harvey Cleckley, *The Mask of Sanity*}

The house is painstakingly detailed in every respect, except
it is a set. No one lives here. No one ever will. The fine veneer

is wasted and beautiful, the paving stones expertly trimmed,
and what's the use, going on? Photographed, this all looks legit.

But that's the crux of this emptiness: there is no way to tell.
Like those Italian mondo movies made before pseudo became fad,

here we have a tribal sex ritual, a polar bear versus a killer whale,
a nudist rebellion, all under English-accented deep-voiced narration

designed to defuse our doubts. The orchid seduces the bee.
And we seduce with a subtler form of mimicry.

ODE TO THE PIPEVINE SWALLOWTAIL

O Singer of Light! O Deep Blue of the Night! You die
to lesson the birds into hunger. And how you live—

burnt-black, orange-embered slugtrosity; a winter holding
in a thin shell; dark wingspan a dead pixel

against a static sky—is not the point, but your northern broods
mimicking northern moods, where each animal dines

on another or dies. O Plated Table! O Airborne Salmonella,
sickness is your trade, as each new-born bird learns,

you give them what they want until their insides burn.
O Stay-Dead Christ, we don't deserve the pain we earn.

ANGEL HEART

Here's to what you never know having done
and so can never admit to. A snake under your skin,
a vein too bold and blue, the visible path

of the heart your father died of. A surgeon
can only work with what she sees, and under the surface
of cut skin is more surface to be cut through.

If you murder you are a murderer,
whether yourself or another. The razor separates you
from your body. This is a litany of violence

no one will remember, given a year or two,
because it is easier to forgive and forget who is responsible
when you are responsible. I am responsible

for the history of the world. The serpent circling us
is the same that twines with its twin to make medicine.
Milk the fangs. Drink the poison.

ODE TO THE LABORATORY FRUIT FLY

O Three-Winged Wonder! O Legs-For-Eyes!
Generations died to shape you, and your children

will die, too, their bodies ground to powder. For Science!
Slavery! What are we researching? Who cares?

Did you know you could be born without a mouth?
Without limbs at all? O Monstrous Sacrifice

to White-Coated Gods, at least your life is short.
Nasty and brutal, yes, but never starved

unless starvation is the study. O Lamb,
your feet bless the ground you stand on,

those stainless tables. O Pull-Apart Victim!
O Soulless Genetic Machinery! O Abattoir!

THE THING

Let me die like a fish, naked to an unfamiliar air.
Let my lungs fill with cotton. Let my head be mounted

to a foreign tongue. Let my unforgiving thoughts
tumor in my brain. Let me be strewn like rain

over the droughted fields. Let all records of my living
be burned in faceless effigy. Let history

forget me. Let swarms of ants dissect my body
and put my flesh to use. Let the hearts and minds

of my children be washed clean of me. Let my genes
be stripped from their genes. Let science invent the methods.

Let philosophers prove I never existed and never could have.
Let tautologies become me. Let me hold you in my arms

because I hold you in my arms because I hold you in my arms.
What have I done? What have I refused? What have I become?

SARAH WINCHESTER

I.

This is the dementia of imagination, a house
for the living built for the dead.

From a distance, a city. Up close, a fingerprint.
O God of Money, God of Guns, here's a temple

to proclaim your name to all the gut-shot
and bleeding-out on the Western plains.

Gardens of corpses bloom fevered ghosts
hunting for their shattered vases, but pretty language

and parquet floors can't stop the staring mirrors,
eyes not your own set like rubies

in the locked bracelet of your face.

II.

The caress of carpet. The hard grasp of ceramic.
Polished wood's punch to the shoulder.

The ragged fingernails of naked brick. Screws like eyes.
Plaster cracks like mouths. A whispering gas jet.

A mocking fire. The boo-hiss of a spit-out ember
on innocent cloth. The breezy accusations.
The settling creaks of condemnation. Oak doors
with their own agenda, sticking in the frame.

The tiled roof always laughing in the rain.

III.

The building must keep building. The hedge maze
must keep growing. The snail must keep losing

itself in the whorls of its shell. If you turn left
in the labyrinth, you will never reach the end.

At the end, in that closed off cul-de-sac,
confronted by that doorless, windowless room,

an empty chair. It begs you to sit
like cool water craves your parched throat.

IV.

A room dedicated to guns. Dedicated guns.
A temple to the trigger pull, the burning powder,

the bullet ingested by the skin. The room echoes
with oiled metal. Ghosts flock to the instruments

which sang their deaths, drawn like ashes
to an urn. The door locked, the key forgotten,

sealed inside, seated on a chair, in a Sunday dress,
Sarah Winchester in effigy, a painted lure

whose painted eyes belie her painted smile.
Enter, my adopted children. Be always at my side.

ABOUT THE AUTHOR

Andrew Kozma received an M.F.A. from the University of Florida and a Ph.D. in English Literature and Creative Writing from the University of Houston. His poems have appeared in *Blackbird*, *The Believer*, *Redactions*, and Bennington Review. and his stories have been published in Analog and *Escape Pod*. His first book of poems, *City of Regret*, was chosen by Richard Jackson for the Zone 3 First Book Award and was published in 2007. At long last, he now considers himself a Texan.

NOTES

These poems first appeared in the following magazines, some in slightly different forms and with different titles:

AGNI: "Ode to the Dying Moth" and "Ode to the Molting Cicada"
Bateau: "Heaven and Earth"
The Believer: "Angel Heart"
Blackbird: "Body Bags" and "Karen Greenlee"
Bodega: "Our Trash and the Trash of Others"
Chariton Review: "Six Years Later, the Memory of the Raw Fish Cubes
    Continues to Haunt Her"
The Cossack Review: "The Thing"
Contemporary Verse 2: "Ode to the Cinnamon-Covered Waxworm" and "Ode
    to the Pipevine Swallowtail"
Isacoustic: "Song of the Coming to Terms With It"
JuxtaProse: "Dark Star (Director's Cut)" and "Ghosts of Mars"
The Kenyon Review: "Ode to the Love Bug" and "Ode to the Male Honeybee"
New Reader Magazine: "As He Had No Issue the Title Became Extinct On
    His Death"
Prairie Winds: "Pulgas Vestidas"
Qualm: "Song of the Self-Righteous," "Song of the Single-Minded," and
    "Into a Mode of Excess"
Red Bird Weekly Read: "Song of the Suicide"
Redactions: "Cigarette Burns" and "Pro-life"
Slab: "Elvis"
The Southampton Review: "Every Snowflake Will Have Its Own Name"

Strange Horizons: "Song of the Ghost Hunter"
Subtropics: "Ode to the Common Housefly"
Third Coast: "Song of the Starving"
Tinderbox: "Song of the Psychopath"
Zone 3: "Tried and Failed"

ACKNOWLEDGMENTS

For encouraging my writing and being first readers, I would like to thank Megan, Tracy Jo, Kelly, Jeylan, Jaime, and Barbara. For continual inspiration and welcome weirdness, I blame Michelle and Martha. For keeping me sane when I'm not writing, I could not do without the friendship of Morgan, Natasha, Afton, Jack, Anne, Bryan, Jason D., and Jason M.

Most of these poems found their original form at a table in Southside Espresso, whose coffee kept me alert and whose staff made me welcome from the day they opened.

Many of these poems were directly inspired by the films of John Carpenter.

CPSIA information can be obtained
at www.ICGtesting.com
Printed in the USA
FSHW021255261021
85660FS

9 781941 462201